GIANT PANDAS

Wildlife Monographs – Giant Pandas
Copyright ©2006 Evans Mitchell Books

Text and Photography Copyright ©2006 Heather Angel

Heather Angel has asserted her rights to be identified
as the author and photographer of this work in
accordance with Section 77 of the Copyright, Designs
and Patents Act 1988

First published in the United Kingdom by:
Evans Mitchell Books
Norfolk Court, 1 Norfolk Road,
Rickmansworth, Hertfordshire WD3 1LA
United Kingdom

Jacket and Book Design by:
Roy Platten
Eclipse
roy.eclipse@btopenworld.com

British Library Cataloguing in Publication Data.
A CIP record of this book is available on request
from the British Library.

ISBN: 1-901268-12-8

10 9 8 7 6 5 4 3 2 1

Pre Press: F.E Burman, London, United Kingdom

Printed in Thailand

GIANT PANDAS

HEATHER ANGEL

Evans Mitchell Books

Foreword

It is a great pleasure for me to introduce this beautiful book on the giant panda, with its stunning collection of photographs by Heather Angel. It is also testament to the work of WWF that I should be invited to do so.

The image of the giant panda – a creature both highly appealing and desperately vulnerable – was adopted as the face of global conservation in 1961 by the founders of WWF. It was an inspired choice, and remains so. At the time, people the world over were captivated by the first pandas being seen outside China, at international zoos. Today, we are no less enamoured with this most reclusive of mammals, which continues to represent the precarious state of many species and environments across the globe.

But, as you will see in this book, there is much room for optimism. During the years that WWF has been working in China, there have been many great breakthroughs for the panda – such as a vast increase in protected reserves, and the planting of bamboo corridors to link the fragmented areas of its habitat, and enable isolated populations of pandas to meet and breed.

As threats such as climate change and China's huge economic development put further pressure on the remaining pandas, it is vital that we understand their needs as fully as possible. Heather's extraordinary work provides a delightful and informative contribution to this body of research. Her spectacular photographs capture a fresh view of the instantly recognisable panda, and present a truly engaging picture of a lifestyle that remains such a mystery to us. It truly is a splendid study of a fascinating animal.

Robert Napier
Chief Executive
WWF-UK

Contents

Introduction   6

History and distribution   10

Distinguishing features   17

Habitat and diet   30

Behaviour and lifestyle   46

Reproduction and   65
growing up

Pandas and people   77

Conservation   84

Information and   96
Acknowledgements

Introduction

The giant panda is one of the world's most endangered mammals, which very few people have seen in the wild. Yet, the unique black and white markings make the panda instantly recognisable from the smallest photograph. Confined to a small part of China, the panda's temperate montane habitat has shrunk so dramatically this enchanting animal needs all the help and protection we can provide.

Wildlife Monographs – Giant Pandas gives an insight to how pandas are adapted to live and survive in China's remote mountainous forests. For the most part of each day, pandas feed on bamboo, so it is difficult to record other aspects of their behaviour. The images here provide an intimate picture of the panda's unique way of life, including rare images of pandas in a winter wonderland.

The charismatic giant panda – recognised the world over as a symbol for conservation – was chosen as the World Wide Fund for Nature's (WWF) distinctive logo from the onset in 1961.

Above: Pausing whilst feeding, a panda looks directly into the camera lens clutching bamboo shoots in each paw with a lone shoot falling from clenched jaws.

Right: An immature giant panda is reflected in a pool as it walks beside the edge of the Pitiao River, Sichuan Province, China.

This book explores the giant panda's habitat and way of life. It also outlines the problems which giant pandas face today. Satellite photographs reveal that between 1974 and 1989, 50 percent of the panda's forest habitat was lost by felling. Also, pandas get caught in poacher's traps set for other animals, which further threatens the precarious natural population.

Read how biologists are working on ways towards restoring the panda habitat in their efforts to aid population recovery. Even though there are now 53 panda reserves in China, some contain only a handful of individual pandas. Recently, panda corridors have been planted to link smaller adjacent reserves to allow intermingling of the panda populations.

WWF was the first international conservation organisation to be invited to work in China. Since 1980, Chinese and Western WWF-sponsored research scientists have been working together with the aim of ensuring the long-term survival of wild populations of a very special animal – the giant panda.

Above: A panda uses its hind limbs and one paw to climb a tree in winter within the forest, while the other holds a branch.

Opposite page, top: A typical feeding stance adopted by a panda is to sit on the ground – here amongst green vegetation – with its feet outstretched. One paw is grasping a bamboo stem, the other a bunch of bamboo leaves it has bitten off from the stem.

Opposite page, bottom left: A giant panda lies down to rest whilst pausing to feed on bamboo. The sky reflection in the eyes defines their small size relative to the conspicuous eye patches.

Opposite page, bottom right: A young panda stands up against a tree after a snowfall in February. In this weather, the black and white colouration disrupts the panda's body shape as the black fur merges with dark trunks and the white fur with the snow.

History and distribution

The giant panda is regarded as China's national treasure. Long before the outside world was aware of the giant panda's existence, the animal was revered by Chinese emperors. Indeed, several thousand years ago, owning a giant panda was regarded as a status symbol because it was extremely difficult to catch one in the wild. Several pandas were therefore included amongst the emperor's menagerie in the Palace Gardens at Xi'an.

In prehistoric times giant pandas ranged over a wide area, extending south of China into north Vietnam and Burma (now Myanmar), as far east as Shanghai and up to Peking (as Beijing was known). When the climate in eastern China became drier and the forests were destroyed for agriculture, pandas were driven further and further north as the bamboo stands diminished in the south. Today, pandas are confined to mountainous regions at elevations between 1200 and 3500 metres (5,000 and 10,000 feet) in Sichuan, Shaanxi and Gansu provinces within south-west China, east of the Tibetan plateau.

Above: Come sun, rain or snow, giant pandas remain active throughout the year. Viewed against a snow blanket, this panda's fur can be seen to be ivory-coloured rather than pure white.

Right: A giant panda sits feeding on bamboo in Wolong Nature Reserve amongst a lush growth of ferns in June. UNESCO declared Wolong an international Biosphere Reserve in 1980. Situated in Sichuan Province, it is a mere 145 kilometres (90 miles) from the vast capital city of Chengdu with a population approaching 10 million.

CHINA

Xi An

Chengdu

Shanghai

Myanmar

Vietnam

Laos

Hong Kong

Thailand

Historic range
of giant pandas

Present giant
panda distribution

The giant panda was unknown to the western world until 1869, when Père Armand David, a French missionary who was also a knowledgeable naturalist, spotted a skin in Sichuan. David realised it was a species new to science and believing it to be a bear, he gave it the scientific name of *Ursus melanoleuca* or black-and-white bear. After the French zoologist, Alphonse Milne-Edwards, examined Père David's specimens, he renamed it *Ailuropoda melanoleuca* in 1870.

Once the panda's existence became known outside China, big-game hunters were eager to bag a panda. Also, museums the world over clamoured to display a stuffed panda, which led to several expeditions to China specifically to hunt pandas. Then the quest was on to find a live panda and bring it back to the west. How this came about is a remarkable story.

Top: Map showing how the historic range of giant pandas extended over most of southern China as well as into Burma (now Myanmar) and Vietnam, compared to the isolated pockets of the present distribution.

Above: During winter, snow falls frequently in Wolong Nature Reserve, but the Pitiao River continues to flow. The river rocks become more clearly defined when coated with snow.

12

When the adventurer William Harkness died in Shanghai before setting eyes on a panda, his widow – Ruth Harkness – decided to carry on with his quest to collect a live panda for the Bronx Zoo in New York. After hosting a cocktail party, this New York socialite set sail for China in 1936. Many people in China tried to discourage her, but there was no going back when Quentin Young, an American-born Chinese hunter, offered to lead her expedition. They left Shanghai in September 1936 sailing up the Yangtse River to Chengdu from where they walked into the Sichuan mountains, trekking through bamboo forests. Rivers could only be crossed by building log bridges and by this time, snow was beginning to fall. But their efforts were rewarded by finding some panda droppings. Later when a hunter fired at a female giant panda she ran off into the forest and squeaks from within a hollow tree trunk led them to a baby panda. Fortunately, Ruth Harkness had brought some feeding bottles and dried milk powder. The infant panda, which Ruth called Su Lin, was carried down the mountain in a bamboo basket, with frequent feeding stops. They sailed together from Shanghai and arrived in San Francisco just before Christmas, providing a wonderful story for the North American press. It was not long before the world outside China fell in love with this new found monochromatic bear.

Above: A giant panda walks along a forest track in winter when the lush herb layer has died down. This low viewpoint shows how the panda's nose is on level with its belly when it walks.

During the decade 1936–1946, fourteen giant pandas were removed by foreigners. After this, China clamped down on the exploitation of pandas from abroad; but between 1957 and 1983 China donated two dozen pandas as goodwill ambassadors to overseas countries. Then China began to loan pandas to overseas zoos under a lucrative rent-a-panda scheme.

Pandas live in remote mountain forest with dense understoreys. The mountainous habitat and inhospitable terrain made it difficult to gain an accurate estimate of the wild giant panda population. Since the 1980's it was estimated some 1000 giant pandas remained in the wild. During the 2000–2004 survey undertaken by researchers using GPS technology, however, individual pandas were painstakingly counted and the total was found there to be almost 1600. Even though this is a 40 percent increase on the previous total, this may be due to more sophisticated means of counting than an actual increase.

The gene pool within individual panda pockets is very limited which further threatens the survival of this charismatic mammal. Small wonder that the giant panda is listed as Critically Endangered in Appendix 1 of the 1973 Convention on International Trade in Endangered Species of Wild Flora and Fauna (CITES).

Above left: The unique white face with black eye patches make the giant panda instantly recognisable even from a tiny black and white photograph

Above right: Baby mammals love to play and giant pandas are no exception. Here, a one-year-old panda cub has climbed onto a moss-covered fallen tree trunk to play in September.

Right: A giant panda stands up within the fork of a tree close to the ground, proving that pandas – in between sitting down to feed – can be quite agile.

Distinguishing features

The giant panda's specific name *melanoleuca*, which means black and white, refers to the distinctive monochromatic coat of this bear-like animal. Viewed head-on the massive head has a large round white face with black eye patches, round black Mickey Mouse-like ears and black marks across the muzzle. Seen from the side, a panda's head has an extended muzzle like a bear.

The rest of the body is white or a dirty cream colour, with a black chest, limbs and feet. The conspicuous black band which runs across the shoulders and connects with the black forelimbs, is seen most clearly when looking down onto a panda from above. A short white furry tail blends in with the white rump and is not at all obvious when flattened against the body protecting the glandular area beneath. The tail is raised up when the panda defecates or when it wants to scent-mark trees.

Left: The massive head of the giant panda has a round white face with black eye patches, nose and ears. The eye patches make the eyes look larger than in reality, which adds to the panda's appeal.

Above: The panda's distinctive black and rounded Mickey Mouse-like ears show up clearly here against snow-covered ground and from certain angles against the white body.

As a panda walks out from the forest into an open clearing, or beside a river, the black and white body is so conspicuous it seems strange it has evolved such a striking colouration. Inside the forest however, the light is dappled with sun and shade, so that a giant panda blends in with the light and shadows. This applies even more so when snow falls in winter and the dark tree trunks break up the uniform white blanket.

Panda legs are short but powerful and, like humans, the plantigrade feet are placed flat on the ground with both the toe and the heel making contact. As it walks, the panda's head is held low with the nose quite close to the ground. The distinct waddling pigeon-toed gait which pandas adopt when ambling through the forest conveys a benign, somewhat lethargic cuddly bear. Yet when alarmed, pandas can break into a trot or even a slow run. On steep slopes, especially after a snowfall, pandas easily loose their footing and end up sliding or even rolling down a hillside. Pandas are also quite capable of defending themselves with a sharp blow from a paw if necessary.

Opposite page, top left: Viewed from below, the giant panda's head can be seen to have an obvious muzzle like other bears.

Opposite page, top right: A conspicuous black band runs across the giant panda's shoulders, breaking up the white expanse of fur as it connects with the black forelimbs.

Opposite page, bottom: A rear view of a giant panda walking through a bamboo glade after a snowfall in winter shows the short white furry tail.

Above: The giant panda's tail becomes much more obvious when it is raised. A newborn panda has a much longer tail in proportion to its tiny body.

Pandas can stand upright on their hind legs but, unlike black bears, they do not walk on them. The forelimbs are often used to prop themselves up against a tree trunk or a large rock. Any of the paws may be used to scratch the body. Forepaws grasp trunks when climbing and help balance when perching on a branch. They are also essential for holding and manipulating bamboo for feeding. In common with other bears, pandas have five fingers, but they also have an extra digit formed from a wrist bone. Known as the pseudothumb, it is used by the panda to deftly manipulate the bamboo. How this is done is explained in more detail in the Feeding Chapter.

Above: Out in an open forest glade, a monochromatic giant panda stands out very clearly amongst green herbaceous plants.

Right: A giant panda walks with its heavy head held low, close to the ground; the lower jaw almost touching the raised fore paw.

Overleaf: A giant panda walks beside a river, stepping deftly from one rock to another.

Left: When walking, a giant panda holds its head below the shoulders as it waddles along with a pigeon-toed gait.

Bottom left: A young giant panda uses its fore limbs to prop itself up against a rock beside a river, in much the same way as a human baby will hold onto a person or furniture when learning to walk.

Bottom right: As a young giant panda approaches a tree trunk, it stands up so it can hug it with the fore limbs.

Opposite page, top: A giant panda looks up as it begins to stand, but moves towards a tree to support itself with a paw against the trunk to stand upright. Unlike bears, pandas cannot walk on their hind feet.

Opposite page, bottom: Giant pandas' bodies are amazingly supple. This animal has twisted its rear body so that a hind paw can reach to scratch its back.

Male pandas are on average about 10 percent larger then females, weighing from 85–125 kilos (187–276 pounds) compared with 70–100 kilos (154–220 pounds) for female pandas. When standing on all fours, a giant panda reaches 70–80 centimetres (27–32 inches) in height at the shoulder and 1.2–1.7 metres (4–5.5 feet) tall when it stands upright on the hind legs only.

Panda outer fur is long and coarse, beneath lies shorter dense woolly under-hair. Together, they not only help to keep the animals warm in the cold winters but also cushion an accidental fall from a tree, should a branch suddenly break. The fur is oily to the touch which helps to repel water and snow. The back hairs are about 4 centimetres (1.6 inches) long, while the shoulder hairs reach 5–7 centimetres (2–2.7 inches) long. All paws have claws which help the panda to grip the trunk when it climbs a tree.

Right: Two giant pandas play-fighting on snow-covered ground use their forepaws to strike the opponent in a harmless way. The effective disruptive black and white colouration can be seen in this sombre winter scene with dark trunks rising up from snow-covered ground.

For many years there has been some dispute as to whether a giant panda was a type of raccoon, like the smaller red or lesser panda, or a bear because it has affinities with both animals. Pandas certainly look like bears, with large bodies and the blood of both is very similar. Their round ears are similar to Asiatic black bears, but unlike bears, giant pandas sit down to feed. Like red pandas (which belong to the raccoon family) giant pandas have wide molar teeth for crushing bamboo. Unlike red pandas they do not live in groups nor do they spend a lot of time up trees. Recent DNA research has proved pandas are indeed bears, which supports Père David's original assumption.

Top left: As a giant panda uses all four limbs to climb a tree, the claws dig into the bark.

Top right: Once a safe branch has been reached, a giant panda will sit on it, using the fore limbs to clasp branches.

Opposite page, top left: The giant panda's thick oily fur is an effective waterproof barrier against rain or snow.

Opposite page, top right: A giant panda using one fore paw to grasp a bamboo stem, whilst the other feeds a bunch of leaves into the side of the mouth.

Opposite page, bottom: Both fore paws – which are larger than the hind paws – of the giant panda are used to hold and manipulate bamboo whilst feeding in a typical half sitting, half lying down pose.

Habitat and diet

Giant pandas once lived much further south in forested riverine valleys, but were forced to move northwards as a result of climate change and forest clearance. They also moved up mountains after the valleys were settled and the forests were felled for growing crops.

Giant pandas now live within mountain ranges at elevations ranging from 1,200–3,400 metres (4,000–11,000 feet). Here, 76–102 centimetres (30–40 inches) of rain and snow fall each year and the peaks are often shrouded with mist and clouds. In the winter, the tops have permanent snow cover, whereas once the sun shines on lower elevations the snow soon melts.

Above: Framed by leafy bamboo shoots, a giant panda clasps the stem to munch the leaves.

Right: Intermittent low cloud and mist, together with a high rainfall maintain a humid environment for most of the year, which encourages a lush growth of wildflowers, shrubs and trees within the temperate mixed forest.

Old growth temperate broadleaf and mixed forests, where bamboo groves flourish beneath larger trees and there is easy access to a stream or river, are favoured by pandas. The water content in older bamboo has to be supplemented with natural water, so that most days pandas need to drink from streams or pools. Lower down the mountains, the forest is mainly deciduous trees – including maples and birches which shed their leaves in winter. Higher up the mountain, tree-like rhododendrons begin to appear and more evergreen conifers. The panda's thick oily coat helps to keep it warm within these damp forests.

Above: A giant panda sits feeding on bamboo in Wolong Nature Reserve with a mountain backdrop behind. Sitting down to feed helps to conserve energy.

Opposite page, top: After a heavy overnight snowfall, a panda sits down on the snow to feed.

Opposite page, bottom: A mixed forest grows right down to the water's edge beside the Pitiao River in Wolong Nature Reserve.

Pandas feed almost exclusively on two kinds of bamboo – arrow *(Sinarundinaria fangiana)* and umbrella *(Fargesia robusta)* – preferring the leaves and shoots, but also eating some stems. Some 99 percent of their diet is bamboo, but they do eat other plants including gentians and irises, also fish and carrion occasionally. Other mammals which are bamboo specialist feeders include the red or lesser panda, the bamboo rat and bamboo lemurs.

In the wild, a giant panda spends 11–14 hours per day chomping on 12–38 kilos (26–84 pounds) of bamboo. Bamboo leaves contain more protein than the stems. The reason why pandas have to eat so much is that they are classified as carnivores and have a carnivorous gut with a short intestine that is not adapted to plant digestion. Their oesophagus does, however, have tough walls to prevent damage from bamboo splinters. Herbivorous cows have microscopic organisms in their gut which aid the breakdown of plant cell walls. Pandas do not have this gut flora so that most of the bamboo passes straight through, as can be seen from the fibrous panda droppings. Indeed, a cow digests 60 percent of the grass it eats, whereas a panda can digest only 12 percent of the bamboo it consumes.

Opposite page, top: A giant panda ambles along a snow-covered track bordered by bamboos in February.

Opposite page, bottom: The branching pattern of a deciduous tree is etched by a light dusting of snow amongst the evergreen neighbouring trees that grow within Wolong's mixed forest.

Top: After a snowfall, giant pandas shake bamboo stems to loosen the snow before starting to eat.

Bottom: Remnants of snow remain on bamboo as a giant panda feeds in February.

Since pandas do not eat continuously and have naps between feeds, they feed on into the night and so need to be able to locate bamboo when it is dark. Although not nocturnal, pandas have slit-like pupils – similar to cats – which enhance their night vision.

Bamboo stems are inspected and sniffed before they are selected for eating. Tough stems are bitten through and removed from the clump. A panda usually sits on the ground when it is feeding with the feet stretched out in front. However, if there is a convenient bank or tree it will loll against it or it may even lie down to feed.

Opposite page, top: A giant panda lolls down amongst ferns before feeding on a bamboo stem.

Opposite page, bottom: As a giant panda relaxes his grip on bamboo, we have a rare glimpse of the underside of the forepaw. At the top are the five digits each ending in a claw and beneath them is the pseudothumb pad which allows the panda to hold and manipulate the bamboo with great dexterity and speed.

Right: Sometimes giant pandas lie down to feed. The bamboo stem is held above the head so the leafy side branches can be bitten off to form a bunch. A paw then holds one end of the bunch as it is eaten; the panda may swap paws to hold the other end of the bunch.

Opposite page, top: During feeding, the giant panda uses its tongue to roll the bamboo leaves into a bundle before they are eaten.

Opposite page, bottom: A young giant panda cub lies down to feed amongst ferns. At this stage, the head appears even larger compared to the size of the body, than an adult panda.

Top: A sequence showing a giant panda sitting up to feed with a bamboo stem held to one side of the head. Notice how both forepaws are repeatedly used to hold and manipulate the bamboo in preparation to feeding. Firstly, the side shoots are bitten off until a sizable bunch is held in the mouth. The bunch is then removed from the mouth and held in a paw so the leaves can be eaten.

Bottom: A giant panda utilises a snow-covered bank to lounge back whilst sitting down to feed after an overnight snowfall.

Top: After feeding, a giant panda uses the large flexible tongue to wipe its nose.

Bottom: A dropping with undigested bamboo leaves, reveals how inefficiently a giant panda digests its staple food.

Opposite page: In winter, giant pandas gain moisture by licking snow.

A panda is a bear which has a special adaptation for feeding on bamboo; indeed an alternative common name is bamboo bear. Humans grasp an object by wrapping a thumb around it, whereas a panda wraps all five digits around one side of a bamboo stem and then pushes a thumb pad – the so-called pseudothumb – against the other side of the stem, pressing it against the pad of its palm. The pseudothumb is formed from a single enlarged and elongated wrist bone known as the radial sesamoid – covered by a black fleshy pad. Unlike the other five digits on a panda's fore paw it does not have a claw.

You need to see a slow motion video to fully appreciate how adept a panda is at working the bamboo stems, utilising the pseudothumb to manipulate the leafy side stalks into the mouth. Here they are bitten off as a bunch of leaves, not unlike a bunch of watercress. The bunch is then removed from the mouth by the other hand and eaten, stalks first, with the leaves protruding from the opposite side of the mouth. The bamboo leaves are rolled up by the tongue.

In essence, a panda is a powerful chewing machine. The large head contains a heavy skull, to which strong chewing muscles are attached that power the jaws containing the outsized flattened molars used for crushing the tough main bamboo stems and chewing the leaves. In the spring, bamboos produce new shoots; being soft they are easier to eat and therefore much favoured by pandas. They also contain 90 percent water, compared with only 50 percent in the older stems.

Bamboos are grasses which grow for many years annually reproducing new shoots or culms by vegetative means. But sexual reproduction is necessary for genetic variety. Depending on the species, after 30 to 80 years growth, bamboo flowers appear – not just on one clump but on all the clumps of the same species within an area. This synchronous flowering is a great survival mechanism for bamboos; because seed-eating wildlife cannot possibly devour the glut of seeds, some will always remain to produce new plants. This is essential for bamboo regeneration, since after flowering and setting seed, bamboo plants die.

Right: A giant panda pauses to drink from a pool beside the Pitiao River, Wolong. Young bamboo shoots contain almost twice as much water as older shoots, but pandas still need to drink virtually every day.

After bamboo die-off it can be five to ten years before the next generation of bamboo plants reach a size which can support a panda population. Mass die-off associated with the synchronous flowering, is therefore yet another factor which threatens the survival of giant pandas. In the past, they were able to amble off to another part of a large forest; but pandas in small forest pockets will starve if all the accessible bamboo dies off and they cannot easily find another source.

In the mid 1970's, 130 giant pandas died from starvation when three different kinds of bamboos died off within a large area and the pandas could not reach an alternative food source.

Attempts have been made to stagger the natural flowering pattern by spraying bamboos to delay the onset of flowering or to stimulate them to flower earlier, but to no avail. It is possible that when the forests were more extensive, bamboo die-off may have been beneficial to pandas by inducing them to migrate to other areas and thereby meet up with other pandas.

Top: The huge round head of a giant panda has several adaptations for constant munching on bamboo. One of these is the outsized chewing muscles for powering the jaws.

Opposite page: A panda cub peers down at the ground from the fork in a tree in winter.

Behaviour and lifestyle

Comparatively little is known about the lifestyle of pandas, since their mountainous terrain makes it difficult for researchers to locate and track them. A few pandas have been fitted with radio collars which aids the researchers.

Until recently, it was thought that giant pandas were essentially solitary animals, living on their own, spending most of the day seeking out and feeding on bamboo, interspersed with periods of rest. New research by biologists, however, has revealed that small groups of pandas share a large territory, meeting up occasionally outside the breeding season.

Right: Giant pandas sit down to feed in all weathers, even when there is snow on the ground.

Opposite page: A panda cub lounges against a rock beside the Pitiao River at Wolong.

Overleaf: Once a panda cub leaves its mother, it leads a fairly solitary life, meeting up with other pandas only occasionally.

As with any mammals, pandas need to communicate with each other. They do this in two ways, by leaving scent calling cards and by emitting a variety of sounds ranging from bleats, growls, honks and chirps to squeals and barks. Pandas scent by spraying urine and by rubbing a musky anogenital gland against trees or rocks. Scenting may be done by a panda walking up to a tree or a rock, raising the tail to smear scent from the scent gland beneath the tail. Male pandas will even resort to doing a head stand against a tree trunk to raise its hind quarters to scent mark higher up a tree, for the higher the pee is placed, the more dominant the signal.

Opposite page: Giant pandas are not very vocal, but they can utter a range of calls, notably when alarmed and when breeding.

Top: A giant panda sniffs the snow-covered ground to check out the scent where another panda has been sitting.

Overleaf, left: A panda scent-marking a rock from a large glandular area beneath the tail.

Overleaf, right: For most of the time, a giant panda walks at a leisurely pace through the forest, seeking out another suitable clump of bamboo or a water source from which to drink.

In response to a friendly interaction, pandas bleat not unlike a lamb or a goat. Rapid opening and closure of the mouth produces an audible chomp, as the teeth meet in a mild defensive threat. Distraught cubs squeal, while adults bark loudly to intimidate enemies. Leopards and jackals will attack weak pandas, but healthy adults are quite capable of defending themselves with powerful swipes of a paw. Panda cubs may be attacked and eaten by wild dogs or dholes and by yellow-throated martens, which are related to weasels. Female pandas are not territorial, but they don't tolerate other females and sub-adults entering the core areas within the area they roam.

Top: A giant panda's amply built body is surprisingly flexible, enabling it to twist and turn in all directions. Here, by twisting the rear end and raising a back leg upwards, a panda can scratch behind an ear with a hind paw.

Right: If the tummy needs scratching, a giant panda simply lies back and uses one of the fore paws.

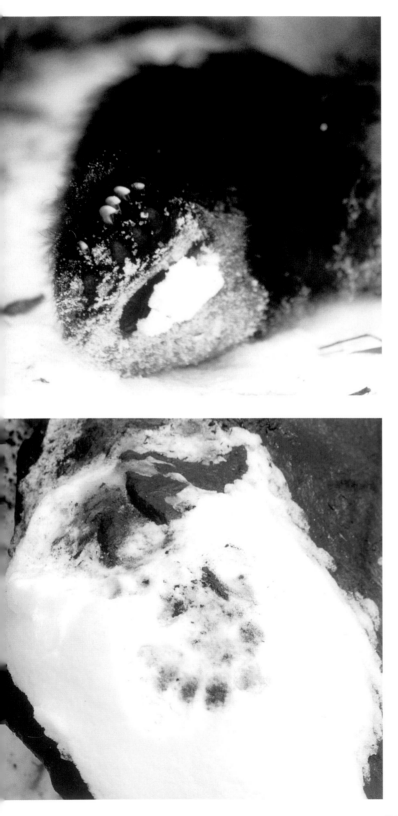

For much of the time pandas amble through the forest at a leisurely pace looking for suitable bamboo clumps and diverting to a stream or river to drink. But giant pandas are also agile tree climbers and can, if necessary, swim across rivers. Their bodies are amazingly supple and will go into strange contortions as they attempt to scratch parts of their body which are difficult to reach.

Wild pandas are typically shy and wary of humans. Once a panda picks up human scent it takes avoiding action by scurrying off into the forest. Pandas are therefore rarely seen in the wild; even by the team who took part in the latest panda survey. Droppings, footprints and evidence of eaten bamboo were found but invariably the trail then went cold. Workers in the survey team collected panda droppings to measure the bamboo shards. Each panda bites bamboo of a given length, which is a useful signature for keeping track of individual pandas.

Top: The underside of a hind paw seen after a panda has been walking in snow. Like the fore paws, it is covered with fur except for a foot pad and the separate digits.

Bottom: Giant panda paw prints show up clearly after a panda has walked on fresh snow, as can be seen on this snow-covered boulder.

Before beginning to climb a tree, a panda stands upright with the fore paws resting on the trunk. As it climbs, claws on their paws help to grip the bark. Indeed, trees that are regularly climbed by pandas have obvious claw marks on the bark. Cubs as young as six months old begin to climb trees where they will swing on horizontal boughs or sit in forked branches to survey their forest home from aloft. Young and older pandas will climb trees to find an elevated place where they can sleep safely.

Right: Trees which are regularly climbed by giant pandas, have obvious scratch marks on the bark made by the strong claws digging in.

Below: When a giant panda wants to climb a tree, it stands up resting the fore paws on the trunk. One foot is raised off the ground and once the trunk is firmly grasped the second foot leaves the ground.

Overleaf, left: A young giant panda relaxes by sitting in the fork of a tree, using a trunk to support its back.

Overleaf, right: Climbing up into the fork of a leafless deciduous tree, a young giant panda gains an elevated view of its forest home in winter.

Pandas can descend trees head or feet first. If need be, pandas can descend quite quickly by sliding bottom-first down the trunk, as a fireman down a pole. Sometimes they fall from trees as dead branches break and fail to support their weight, but their thick fur helps to cushion a fall.

Even though pandas have thick and heavy bones for their size, their bodies are surprisingly flexible, enabling them to twist and turn in all directions. They enjoy somersaulting, especially youngsters on a snow blanket.

Top: All four limbs are used to grip the trunk as a giant panda descends a tree head first.

Below: A giant panda using both hind and fore paws to grasp a trunk as it descends a tree backwards, in a similar fashion to the way a fireman slides down a pole.

Right: A year-old captive-bred panda plays with a leafy twig which it has pulled off a branch of a fallen tree.

Unlike brown bears, pandas do not hibernate in winter. Their restrictive bamboo diet provides enough energy to keep them going on a day-to-day basis, but it is not nutritious enough to lay down fat reserves to fuel pandas during a hibernation period. So, regardless of the weather, pandas have to keep munching on bamboo. During winter months, when there are heavy snow falls at higher elevations, pandas move down the mountain to live and feed at lower levels where the temperatures are slightly higher. Failing this, they can gain some protection curled up at the base of a tree and when the ground is hard or frozen, pandas may use their paw as a pillow when they sleep. During bad weather, they may shelter inside a den.

Left: If a giant panda rolls onto its back or falls on it from a tree, it simply rights itself by rolling onto one side using an arm and a leg to lever up its body.

Right: When walking up snow-covered slopes, a giant panda may lose its balance and roll downhill on its back with all four limbs in the air. Younger pandas love sliding and will retrace their tracks for a repeat slide.

Reproduction and growing up

Female wild giant pandas are able to reproduce when they are four to five years old. They give birth once every two years until they reach about 20 years of age, so that a mother produces only some five to eight cubs during her lifetime. A female is in oestrus or 'on heat' for one to three weeks but is receptive to mating for only three days. Even though natural panda populations are sparse, the breeding potential of wild pandas is comparable with American black bear populations. During the time a female panda is on heat she is attracted to scent calling cards left by males and a mutual exchange of special mating calls, including barks and bleats, echo through the forest. If a female attracts more than one male, they may have to confront one another.

Left: As a mother giant panda stands guard over her captive-bred four-month-old cub, it looks reassuringly at her face.

Above: A year-old captive-bred panda cub stands up on a fallen tree showing the well developed claws on the hind paws.

Pandas mate in the spring anytime from March to May when they make chirping sounds. The male then leaves the female and takes no part in the upbringing of their offspring. Just before a mother panda gives birth she seeks out a large hollow tree or a cave – preferably with bamboos close at hand – as a natural maternity den in which to give birth. Here her newborn cub gains protection from bad weather during the first three months of its life. In Sichuan Province, panda dens tend to be in trees, whereas in the Qinling Mountains mothers utilise stone caves. Many suitable tree dens were lost when big trees were selectively felled.

The mother gives birth – usually to a single cub – five months after mating, as early as August or as late as October. The gestation period during which the baby panda develops inside the mother's uterus varies from 129–160 days (on average it is 147 days) due to the delayed implantation of the embryo. Sometimes a mother gives birth to twin cubs, but only rarely do both survive and typically she rears the firstborn. Very occasionally, three cubs are born, but early deaths can occur by the mother accidentally crushing a tiny newborn which drops from a paw as she sleeps.

Immediately after her baby is born, a mother panda cradles her helpless cub in her arms, holding it close to one of her four nipples. A newborn panda is not at all appealing. The pink baby is covered with fine white hair and is blind. With a tail, it looks more like a baby rat than a panda. Weighing in at just 90–130 grams (3–5 ounces) a giant panda baby is a mere 1/900th the size of its mother. Like marsupials – such as kangaroos – a giant panda baby is one of the smallest newborn mammals relative to its mother's size. Indeed, it easily becomes hidden beneath a mother's forepaw.

Opposite page: As the short winter days lengthen, the season turns to spring and giant pandas meet up to mate during March to May.

Left: A giant panda mother sits to nurse her captive-bred four-month-old cub and will often continue feeding on bamboo.

A mother sits down to allow her cub to suckle, which a newborn may do six to twelve times a day. It takes six to eight weeks before the cub opens its eyes, so that until then it feels and scents its way to the teats. When hungry, a young cub cries like a human baby. Black fur begins to appear in the same places as the adult when it is three weeks old. Panda cubs do not crawl until they are three months old, so that if a mother wants to move her young cub she will pick it up by gently holding the skin above the neck in her teeth, in much the same way as a cat will carry a kitten. Biologists now know that mothers will often leave their cubs for up to 50 hours while they go off to find food. Natural predators of young unattended cubs include leopards, Asiatic wild dogs or dholes and yellow-throated martens. Mothers consume droppings produced by their cub to remove all trace of smell which predators would detect. During the period 1983–87 more than 30 panda cubs, thought to have been abandoned by their mothers, were misguidedly taken from the wild into captivity.

Opposite page, top: A giant panda mother reassures her captive-bred four-month-old cub by patting its back.

Opposite page, bottom: A captive-bred four-month-old giant panda cub snoozes up against its mother's body in-between feeds in January.

Left: Virtually a year after it was born, a giant panda cub enjoys playing on a fallen tree trunk, peering through the forked branches and over the top of the upper one.

Panda cubs continue to feed on their mother's milk for eight to nine months, although they start to eat bamboo snacks when six months old. They are weaned off milk when a year old, but the cubs remain with their mother until they reach 18–30 months. Therefore, a wild panda mother reproduces every other year. This slow breeding rate means that wild panda populations cannot quickly recover from sudden losses due to bamboo die off, habitat loss or illegal hunting.

By the time the cubs are seven months old, like all baby animals they enjoy playing on their own and with one another. Whether it be climbing trees, sliding down slopes, frolicking in the snow or play-fighting with one another, this all helps to enhance their survival skills when they eventually lead an independent life. They also begin to explore their territory, making forays into the forest on their own. At first these are short, but gradually the distance increases as they get to know familiar landmarks, such as a stream, a large rhododendron tree or a fallen trunk. After cubs leave their mothers, they tend to live alone, but it is now known that they may meet up with other pandas from time to time.

Where only a handful of pandas exist in a reserve the gene pool is small, but one way in which this can be enhanced is by planting bamboo corridors linking reserves, thereby tempting pandas to move from one area to another.

Top left and centre: A cub walks along a fallen trunk, slips and hangs precariously by its claws only to end up dropping to the forest floor.

Left: A giant panda cub lies down amongst ferns absorbed in playing with two bamboo stems.

Opposite page: As giant panda cubs grow, they climb higher up trees until they find a convenient fork in which to play or take a nap.

Above: Two giant panda cubs
enjoy frolicking on soft,
snow-covered ground.

Initially, attempts to breed pandas in captivity had a very poor success rate. The first captive-born panda cub Ming Ming, was bred at Beijing Zoo in 1963. It took some time to establish the correct milk formula to give the young pandas and it was also discovered they needed to be kept within a humid environment in the incubator. A total of 161 captive panda cubs have been raised which equals approximately ten percent of the total wild population. None have yet been introduced to the wild.

Captive pandas often live longer than wild animals, but they nonetheless have a poor record for mating and reproducing. Even when cubs are born many do not survive. Jing Ji from Sichuan Province, produced an astonishing total of 14 cubs in captivity, none of which survived. In recent years, however, the success rate has increased. In an attempt to encourage captive pandas to increase their interest in sex and successfully mate, biologists have tried some novel approaches. In the 1990's, captive male pandas were given Chinese medicine to increase the chance of a successful mating. This did improve their sex drive, but it also made the males aggressive so that they attacked the females. In 2001, the anti-impotence drug Viagra, was given to a 16-year-old male panda at Wolong, without effect, but some biologists argue he was just too old.

Screening of panda 'porn' videos of pandas mating, to get them in the mood, proved to be more successful. Hua Mei born at San Diego Zoo in the United States in 1999 was returned to China in February 2004. There she was shown videos of pandas mating before she was introduced to male pandas on 'blind dates'. The result was she became pregnant and gave birth to twin boy cubs later the same year.

If captive pandas do not mate naturally during the very short time a female is on heat, she may be fertilised by means of artificial insemination (AI). This avoids losing a whole year before a panda can become pregnant again. At the Giant Panda Breeding Centre in Wolong, to avoid disturbing mothers and babies, researchers use 24-hour video monitors to observe the way captive baby pandas react to their mothers and how often they feed.

Because the gestation period of captive panda mothers is only 84–160 days and cubs can be hand-raised after they have been weaned at a year, female captive pandas can reproduce once a year.

Left: Like youngsters the world over, giant panda cubs utilise natural objects to play with. Bark stripped from a tree kept this cub occupied for many minutes.

The first panda studbook was published in 1970, listing the parents of captive panda births and their survival rate. The 1999 panda studbook reveals only 28 percent of captive adult pandas were breeding. However, in recent years, there has been an increase in the survival rate of captive born cubs. In 2003, as a result of 29 captive pandas mating by natural or artificial means worldwide, 19 cubs were born, two of which were stillborn and one died later. This gave a survival rate of 84 percent.

After the successful cloning of Dolly the sheep, newspaper articles appeared suggesting that producing cloned pandas would help to save the demise of the giant panda. In truth, the only feasible way to reduce the risk to any endangered species is to conserve the natural population as well as the habitat.

Right: A young giant panda learning about its environment by sniffing the leaves of a shrub. Japanese anemones are in flower behind.

Pandas and people

There are many reasons why giant pandas are regarded with great affection by young and old alike, attracting huge crowds both inside and outside China. Firstly, there is the big face with outsized eyes; although in reality the eyes are not very large, the black eye patches set within the white fur enhance their apparent size. Secondly, captive pandas bumbling along appear as cuddly black and white teddy bears. This is another illusion, since the outer fur is not soft but quite coarse and oily. The endangered status of pandas also helps to generate the pandemonium and extensive press coverage associated with any new panda arrival at a zoo or a breeding centre.

Opposite page: One-year-old captive-bred panda cub plays on a moss-covered fallen trunk.

Above: A child poses for a photograph beside an outsized model giant panda at Beijing Zoo, China. Chinese children adore pandas which can be seen at several zoos in their country.

The Chinese name for the giant panda is *daxiongmao* meaning 'large cat-bear' from the cat-like slit pupils to the eyes. How pandas gained their black markings is recounted in a delightful Tibetan proverb. Originally, pandas were white all over. After a young panda befriended a young shepherdess, a leopard pounced on the panda cub. The young girl defended it, only to be killed by the predator. Several pandas came to her funeral when a local custom of respect was to blacken the arms with ashes. The pandas wept for the shepherdess and as they wiped their eyes with their blackened paws, covered their ears to deaden the sobs of other pandas and hugged each other, the black ashes turned their fur black. Thereafter, pandas had black eyes, ears, arms and legs.

As is the case with many other threatened animals, the reason why giant pandas are now endangered is chiefly due to man destroying their natural habitat, although climate change is another factor. As man demolished their forest home, pandas became extinct in most of their southern distribution areas, shrinking into small pockets in the northern mountainous regions. But even here they were not safe, as logging cleared the forests at lower elevations and selectively felled large trees so essential for maternal panda dens.

Opposite page: A giant panda relaxes sitting on a conifer branch in the forest within Wolong Nature Reserve.

Top: Farmers' houses on either side of the Pitiao River, Wolong. In one, dried maize or corn cobs are hanging under the eaves. A narrow cable bridge connects both sides of the river. Snow defines the roofs and also the areas in the mixed forest which have been cleared for agriculture.

Above: Corn hanging up outside farmer's house in Wolong village in winter, is used to feed pigs.

When bamboo die-off occurs the pandas tend to move down the mountainside in search of more food, only to find their natural forest runs out. They then move onto farmers' land, where they may eat corn or wheat, both of which – like bamboos – belong to the grass family. In the past, if farmers found pandas destroying their crops they would not hesitate to kill them.

Poaching was also a problem. The highly inflated prices a panda pelt can fetch in Hong Kong proved too tempting. In 1988 Chinese officials discovered 146 panda pelts in Sichuan province. The attitude of the Chinese authorities then toughened when they imposed the death penalty on anyone convicted of killing a giant panda. Indeed, when two men were caught at the Chinese border with giant panda and golden monkey pelts in 1996, they were both given death sentences. But only a year later the penalty was changed to a 20 year prison sentence and in 1998 a farmer was convicted of killing three pandas.

Now that pandas are fully protected, attitudes are changing. Farmers no longer hunt pandas and, since many believe pandas bring them good luck, they will provide food for starving animals and may even make a journey up the mountain to collect bamboo. In recent years the Chinese Government has provided an added incentive to protect an injured or lost giant panda with a generous reward.

Top: After working in the fields, a woman returns to her house in Wolong with livestock fodder.

Bottom: A Chang minority grandmother with her grandson outside their wooden farmhouse, Wolong in Sichuan Province.

The panda's plight is inextricably linked with the villages adjacent to the reserves. The quest for natural products used in Chinese traditional medicine impacts on pandas. The traps set by poachers within the forest for musk deer (for musk pods), bears (for gall) and deer (for antlers) also destroy some pandas when they become accidentally caught in snares. Local inhabitants cook and heat their homes with wood fires which are fuelled by felling forest trees. This is why education and guiding local people towards alternative livelihoods, other than poaching or logging, is such an essential part of the panda conservation jigsaw. WWF, together with the Chinese Government, are working together on a costly ten year plan to create new panda reserves and to relocate 10,000 loggers and farmers. Meanwhile, when farmers can no longer survive by hunting or collecting wood for fuel, other livelihoods have to be found. One example is in Laoxincheng Reserve in the Qinling Mountains, where traditional log bee hives, which had to be renewed each year, have now been replaced by WWF providing hives made from wood boards. These have two advantages over the traditional hives in that they last for several years and many more hives can be made from a single tree.

Top: A painting on wooden boarding at a kiosk at Wolong, depicts giant pandas within their mountain habitat, with a mother panda and her new baby, bamboo, flowering rhododendron and pine tree.

The giant panda is such an iconic animal it is used repeatedly for advertising all manner of products in China – including beer and cigarettes. Giant pandas were trained as performing circus animals, but this practice has now been banned.

Top: A giant panda painting by a five-year-old Chinese girl, Luo Si, from Chengdu, the city nearest to Wolong. Hopefully giant pandas will still be around for future generations of children to be motivated to paint them.

Bottom: Chinese artists have for long been inspired to depict giant pandas in their traditional ink brush paintings. This statue, at Wolong, depicts a giant panda family – mother, father and baby.

Opposite page: Omnivorous mammals modify their diet according to the season; for example, brown bears feast on salmon and on berries in autumn. Imagine the tedium of eating just one kind of food, which is essentially what giant pandas do, day in day out. This panda is taking a stroll before tucking in to yet another bamboo meal.

Conservation

It is vital that the panda's habitat be maintained – not just for wild pandas to survive – but also for the successful reintroduction of captive-bred pandas. The mountain forests, where pandas roam, contain the greatest diversity of both plant and animal species found within temperate latitudes; so by conserving these forests, a whole galaxy of species will be saved.

Other animals which share the panda's habitat include the much smaller red or lesser panda *(Ailurus fulgens styani)*, which is related to raccoons. Another subspecies, *Ailurus fulgens fulgens*, lives in the Himalayas. The lesser panda spends much more time up trees than giant pandas, descending to eat bamboo as well as insects, bird eggs and baby birds when they can find them. In cold weather, red pandas wrap the long furry tail around their body to insulate them like a duvet.

Above: A red or lesser panda *(Ailurus fulgens styani)* shares the same habitat as the giant panda. This subspecies is not confined to Sichuan Province, it also occurs in Yunnan Province and in Myanmar. The black underside can be seen when a red panda stands up.

Right: A giant panda grips the trunk with the hind legs as it perches on a slender branch in a coniferous tree.

A troop of golden snub-nosed monkeys *(Rhinopithecus roxellana)* moving through the forest is a spectacular sight, as flashes of rich orange fur are glimpsed between the trees. Adults sport a blue ring around each eye and the males also have blue scrota. Although not quite as endangered as giant pandas, these golden monkeys are classified as vulnerable and are still hunted for their pelts. Their fur was once so esteemed it was worn by Manchu officials. Other parts of the golden monkey's body are used in Chinese traditional medicines.

Clouded leopards *(Neofelis nebulosa)*, the Sichuan takin *(Budorcas taxicolor tibetana)* which is a goat antelope – but misleadingly known as a golden-fleeced cow, musk deer *(Moschus chrysogaster)* and several kinds of resplendent pheasants also live in the same forests as the pandas. In spring, the green slopes are punctuated with a variety of colourful flowering indigenous rhododendrons.

For more than two decades, the WWF has invested a huge amount of time and money towards panda conservation. Working in conjunction with the Chinese Ministry of Forestry, the number of panda reserves has increased from just four in the early 1960's to 53 in 2005. But only some 60 percent of the total panda population actually lives in reserves. Pandas living outside these protected areas are threatened by poaching and habitat loss or fragmentation.

The smallest reserves contain as few as ten pandas. For large mammal species the minimum viable population is thought to be around 50 individuals, so that fragmented panda populations are threatened still further by inbreeding which may lower their resistance to disease.

Opposite page: A red or lesser panda – also known as firefox and red cat-bear – feeding on bamboo. Unlike the giant panda it has a large tail. This is used to keep warm when it curls up to sleep in the fork of a tree in winter at elevations from 2200–4800 metres (7200–15,750 feet). Red panda mothers usually give birth to twins.

Top left: A male golden snub-nosed monkey (*Rhinopithecus roxellana*) bares his teeth in a mild threat. Notice the conspicuous blue eye patches and the curious snub nose.

Top right: Golden snub-nosed monkeys are endemic to mountain forests in south-west China, where they live an arboreal existence, leaping with great agility from one tree to another. The young monkeys have much paler fur than the golden adults as shown by this youngster caught mid leap using his long tail as a rudder.

For years, the planting of bamboo corridors or panda highways to link up isolated pockets has been discussed. In 2003, the Shaanxi Provincial Government in association with WWF, declared five new panda reserves, as well as five bamboo corridors to link up fragmented reserves. To date, six have been planted in Shaanxi with a mix of bamboos and other native plants – notably pines as bamboo requires shade to flourish. The corridors have shown an increase in biomass, with other plants colonising them and more wildlife movements. In 2005 there was evidence that pandas were using the Jiuchi corridor, which is an encouraging sign. They will be able to move from one area to another when their food supply ceases as a result of bamboo die-off and also allow genetic exchange between pandas.

Opposite page, top: An azure-winged magpie *(Cyanopica cyana)* feeds on a pheasant road kill beside the road north of Wolong village in winter. Small flocks of these long-tailed birds can often be seen flying through the forest.

Opposite page, bottom: The golden pheasant *(Chrysolophus pictus)* is but one of several kinds of ornamental pheasants endemic to China. The male has a much more colourful plumage than his drab mate.

Top: Farmers' houses at Wolong in June with a potato crop in the foreground.

Right: A giant panda – one of two rented from China for 10 years – relaxing in an air-cooled grotto at the National Zoo in Washington DC, USA. Panda cams have been set up here for observing the panda activity at the zoo.

Giant pandas have always proved the star attraction at any zoo. In response to the many short term loans of giant pandas – including the pair which came to the Los Angeles zoo for the 1984 Olympics – the US Fish and Wildlife Service banned the import of giant pandas to the USA in 1993. Conservation bodies have never been in favour of short term loans. Quite apart from additional threats to wild and captive panda populations, they felt that long air flights could be stressful to the pandas. In 1996, on the strength of their research programme, San Diego Zoo was granted a permit to import a pair of giant pandas for US $1million per year for a ten year breeding loan. This loan was granted on the condition that the funds are used for giant panda conservation – including both habitat protection or captive breeding – and that any cubs born would belong to China and be returned there after they were three years old. Hua Mei, born in 1999 was returned to China in 2004.

Giant pandas can be seen in the USA at the Smithsonian National Zoological Park in Washington DC, San Diego Zoo, Zoo Atlanta and Memphis Zoo.

This page: Captive-bred giant panda cubs develop their climbing skills by playing on a climbing frame – part of the enrichment equipment within the enclosure at the Wolong Breeding Centre.

Opposite page: Young pandas enjoy frolicking by somersaulting over each other, especially when the ground is cushioned with snow.

Television is but one of many ways to educate people, both inside and outside China, about the plight of the panda. The thinly dispersed wild panda populations make filming difficult, but the British wildlife cameraman Michael Richards, filmed pandas for the BBC film entitled *Bears – Spy in the Woods*, in part by an innovative method whereby pandas took their own footage. Four small cameras, known as 'bamboo cams', were each hidden inside a large bamboo stem beside ridge paths which pandas use as their highways in the Qinling Mountains in Shaanxi Province. The cameras were triggered by a passing panda activating an infra-red sensor, in a similar way to the device used with automated doors that open as you walk towards them.

Opposite page: A young giant panda climbs a tree and rests its body against a small trunk hugging it with the forearms.

Top: Three captive-bred giant panda cubs sit together in harmony as they feed in their enclosure at Wolong Breeding Centre.

It is a sobering thought to realise that from 1936–1999, a total of 467 giant pandas have been kept in captivity. The current figure is approaching 200, which equals ten percent of the total wild population. Ultimately giant pandas will not survive by increasing the number of captive animals. Experts have been debating about the pros and cons of reintroduction of pandas to the wild since 1999. There is talk that 2005 will see this become a reality. If an initial reintroduction is successful, the pandas stand a chance of surviving in the long term.

Let us hope for a positive outcome from all the money and effort now being poured into saving the giant panda; for quite simply, to contemplate the demise of the beloved panda is unthinkable.

Top: A captive young panda uses its hind feet to hold a bamboo stem in readiness whilst feeding on leaves.

Opposite page: The long term destiny of giant pandas cannot be predicted. Hopefully we have not left it too late to save this charismatic species for future generations to enjoy.

Information and Acknowledgements

Information

Internet sites
More information about pandas can be found on the following websites.

Arkive
A digital library of photographs, film clips and information on endangered species – including the giant panda. http://www.arkive.org

National Geographic Society
http://www.nationalgeographic.com

San Diego Zoo panda cam
http://sandiegozoo.org/pandas/pandacam/index.html

Smithsonian National Zoological Park, Washington, USA.
Giant pandas site with panda cam
http://nationalzoo.si.edu/Animals/GiantPandas/

World Wild Fund for Nature – China
http://www.wwfchina.org/english

World Wide Fund for Nature – UK
http://www.wwf.org.uk

World Wildlife Fund – worldwide
http://www.worldwildlife.org

Acknowledgements

Many people helped in the production of this book. I should especially like to thank Director Zhang Hemin of the Wolong Centre for the Conservation and Research of the Giant Panda and his staff for assistance with photography, and WWF-China for up-to-date information. In Great Britain, WWF-UK and the Zoological Society of London also helped to provide information. I am greatly indebted to Robert Napier, Chief Executive of WWF-UK, for writing the Foreword and to my staff: Justin Harrison who meticulously scanned all the transparencies, Valerie West who produced the final copy and Kate Carter who proof read the book.

Note: in the United States and Canada, the WWF is known as the World Wildlife Fund; elsewhere it is known as the World Wide Fund for Nature. Throughout this book these have been abbreviated to simply WWF.

Other titles in this series include:

Elephants by Dr Tracey Rich & Andy Rouse
ISBN: 1-901268-08-X

Cheetahs by Dr Tracey Rich & Andy Rouse
ISBN: 1-901268-09-8

Sharks by Jonathan Bird
ISBN: 1-901268-11-X

Leopards by Fritz Pölking
ISBN: 1-901268-12-8